Groups and Group Dynamics: Contact in the Intergroup and Prejudice

EDOARDO
ZELONI MAGELLI

ISBN: 978-1-80111-647-3

Original Edition: October 2010 *"Gruppi e Dinamiche di Gruppo: Il Contatto nell'Intergruppo e il Pregiudizio*

First English Edition: February 2018

Author:

Psychologist, Entrepreneur and Consultant
Edoardo Zeloni Magelli, was born in Prato in 1984.

In 2010, soon after graduating in Psychology of Work and Organizations, he launched his first startup. As a Businessman he is CEO of Zeloni Corporation, a training company specialising in Business Applied Mental Sciences. His company is a reference point for anyone who wants to realize an idea or a project. As a scientist of the mind he is the father of Primordial Psychology and helps people to strengthen their minds in the shortest possible time. A music and sport-lover.

UPGRADE YOUR MIND → zelonimagelli.com

UPGRADE YOUR BUSINESS → zeloni.eu

It's not only books under fire now that worry me.
It is the books that will never be written.
The books that will never be read.
And all due to the fear of censorship.
As always, young readers
will be the real losers.

Judy Blume

Censorship is the child of fear
and the mother of ignorance.

Laurie Halse Anderson

Dedicated to those who censored
my university thesis:
"The Theory of Reality"

*Without your censorship
this text would never have been written*

A special thanks to the students
who witnessed the censorship
of my university thesis:
"The Theory of Reality"

*When you observe puppets,
you understand how wonderful it is
to think differently, move differently
and feel different things.*

CONTENTS

Ψ

ABSTRACT

Prejudice is a subject that has aroused great interest in human and social sciences, because it refers to environments and problems - such as the relationship with diversity, discrimination, civil society, peace, cross-cultures - of extreme theoretical, practical and political relevance. This interest has intensified since the Second World War, in relation to the discriminatory programs that developed around totalitarian ideologies, the important forms of racism that have affected the United States of America and in the recent important migration phenomenon in Europe. According to the Contact hypothesis (Allport, 1954), if the meeting between members of different groups takes place under favorable conditions, it can reduce prejudice.

In the last 20 years, some theoretical models, which derive from the theory of social identity

(Tajfel, 1981), have proposed to expand the hypothesis of contact in particular to identify the conditions that lead to the generalization of the positive effects of contact from familiar outgroup members (proximal outgroup) to non-familiar outgroup members (distal outgroups). There are negative factors such as anxiety, authoritarianism and regulatory restrictions that deserve more attention because they can become key points for the future search for intergroup contact. Such an emphasis would allow a more complete understanding of the conditions that increase and inhibit the potential positive effects of contact.

Rather than placing contact in a situational phenomenon, it needs to be placed in a social, multi-level and longitudinal context.

A group of people
who share a common goal
can achieve the impossible.

Anonym

If the ants are all in agreement,
they can move an elephant.

Proverb of Burkina Fasu

1

THE SOCIAL GROUP

In sociology and social psychology, a group is defined as a number of people who interact with each other in an orderly manner based on shared expectations regarding their respective behavior. It is a group of people whose status and roles are interrelated. Since human beings are basically animals that have an aptitude to cooperate, groups are a vital part of the social structure. Groups are formed and transformed constantly; they do not need to be self-defined and are often identified from the outside. Groups are held together by so-called cohesion, that is, by the intensity of the relationship between the members in each group. Cohesion is determined by many factors, among which, mutual attraction, (that is, the members feel attraction towards each other) or identification, when a member identifies with the group.

Why are groups formed? Groups are a fundamental part of our lives: we are born in a group, that is, the family. In the classroom we learn as a group, we play in groups. Since man has walked the earth, he has always lived in a group. In a group we can satisfy both our biological and psychological needs, which can't be satisfied on our own. Therefore, the group aims to improve the survival of the individual. Social evolutionist psychologists say that natural selection does not favor those who live in isolation, but those who live in groups. A group of people is a group of individuals who meet and have common goals that are more or less declared and explicit. The individual has physical, psychological, aptitude, behavioral, relational, emotional and sentimental characteristics inside, which are determined by his past history, the present situation and future expectations.

We can define this person as a complex unit and add that he/she also has the peculiarity of having the dynamic ability to change him or herself and change the surrounding environment. The degree of plasticity that each person possesses varies greatly and can range from a minimum capacity of change to maximum willingness.

What is the sound
of one hand clapping?

Koan Zen

It takes two flints
to make a fire.

Louisa May Alcott

2

GROUP DYNAMICS

The concept of group dynamics has been introduced in psychology by Kurt Lewin to indicate relationships that affect a group and that influence its development and behavior. An academic who originally belonged to the school of thought that refers to the theory of Gestalt, speculates that the system of relations and communication that characterizes a group can be considered as a sort of **"field"**, in which forces are distributed and focus, not casually, on following trends related to balance and tensions connected to membership life.

Inside a group, or within subgroups, ties that are subject to change are established and derive from the interference between individual conditions, the characteristics of each participant, and of the group, due to social interactions and interpersonal perceptions. The dynamics of the Group therefore proposes to analyze the progress of the group's relationships, its structure and its flow. Even though the contributions offered by various authors (after Lewin) made the problem much more complex and introduced interpretative principles which were sometimes very distant from each other: such as social-metric and psychoanalytic ones, for example, we can say that it is possible to highlight a series of common dispositions that are found within each group.

By the term group dynamics, we mean the evolution of relationships in the group. Tuckman (1965) proposed a **model of group life evolution** consisting of five sequential phases:

- Forming

The members of the group are oriented and understand what the behavior should be towards the coordinator and the other members.

- Storming

There is a climate of hostility towards the other members of the group and/or towards the leader, especially due to uncertainty, lack of directives and psychological support, because of the lack of rules and resistance to the structure. Emotional resistance develops when a task needs to be performed as an expression of one's own unwillingness.

- Norming

Members accept each other, and group rules are developed to which everyone feels committed to.

- Performing

The members of the group accept their role and work to achieve the agreed goals.

- Adjourning

The members of the group decide to put the activities on hold in order to evaluate the modus operandi and the results obtained.

Group cohesion defines the level of solidarity among its members, but also the sharing of rules and the respective sense of belonging. This cohesion is also determined by many emotional factors. By the expression **dynamic group processes** we are instead referring to the relational and emotional dynamics that take place in therapy groups (the concept is especially used in the Analytical-Group area). Now we will see how the group, considered as a whole, behaves on a level of main dynamics in its various stages of life, similar to what happens in a living organism, and that we can find in almost all groups.

The first movement concerns **the birth of the group** that transforms its members and the external context in an attractive, yet repulsive at the same time. There is a fluctuation between desire and fear. The desire for novelty, for the exchange between equals, for the creation of a new subject, for possible solidarity and for the mutual increase of strength to carry out the activities. The fear is of the inevitable change that will be take place of the group in the members and in the context, and that will produce moments of insecurity and crisis requiring a certain effort to overcome them.

Another important dynamic is **growth** intended as the strengthening and refining of skills, the increase of self-confidence, the search for satisfaction with one's own independence. Every fluctuation of growth puts the group in front of change, that is, in the hypothesis of advancing and that of breaking down. Every role and every rule that only one member tries to change requires the questioning of the whole set-up of the group.

The dynamic that almost constantly crosses the path of a group is **the movement between differentiation and harmony.** The group is a number of diversities that on one hand seek harmony and sharing but, on the other hand, want to maintain, through differentiation, the characteristics of the individuals, their identity. The movement of the group will be towards the highest degree of integration and differentiation, increasing unity and at the same time enhancing individual singularities.

With **a decision** we are confronted with one of the most difficult movements because the choice of one thing means the exclusion of another. Since choices are made according to options proposed by individuals, it is possible to understand how exclusion feeds the feeling of guilt and the consequent inadequacy with respect to the other members of the group. The effort to prevent a creative decision that includes all options is very difficult if not impossible.

The dynamic of **action**, understood as the movement for the implementation of a task, is a moment in which the group is confronted with reality. On the emotional level we have a state of tension together with fear, that is, the desire to carry out the activity accompanied by the desire to escape it.

With the dynamic of the **mirror** the group has the possibility to reflect upon itself, in an action and interaction mode. It takes a good level of emotional strength, self-confidence and self-esteem to face reality, to look at oneself in the mirror. The risk that lies behind this dynamic is represented by excessive self-criticism or excessive self-satisfaction. Between the extremes of "nothing is good" to "we are too good", we must be able to objectively identify the strengths and weaknesses of the group, and the leader, in this case, it can play an important role as an external observer to balance the effects.

Lastly, are **the defenses** that the group, but also the individuals, carry out to control, slow down or stop a process of change. Normally defenses are an indicator of good health, but when they become constant and insistent they can cause suffocation and paralysis in the group or of its members. It is not so much a matter of breaking down the defenses, because this would entail the escape of the members from the group or their further closure, but rather to make them evident, explicit and become aware of them in order to give the group the possibility and the freedom to overcome them. Depending on the type of fear we can use various defensive mechanisms both for the group and individually.

Fig.1 **The Group Dynamic** *(Zeloni Magelli, 2010)*

It's harder to crack
prejudice than an atom.

Albert Einstein

Be kind, always,
for everyone you meet
is fighting a harder battle.

Plato

3

PREJUDICE

Prejudice is a mental strategy, a simplification, a distortion of reality, and it is a social phenomenon rooted in the regulatory system of society. It is the attitude of a social group towards another group, based solely on their group membership. Imagine that you are told that next semester you will share a room with a student from Great Britain, or from France, or from Saudi Arabia, or from Israel. The simple fact of knowing that your new roommate comes from a specific country tends to trigger in you certain attitudes based on certain beliefs of what that person will be like (the British are reserved, the French have an artistic sensibility, the Americans are serious and enterprising and so on). Some of these attitudes will be positive, others negative.

Although prejudice seems to be universal, in some respects it varies from one culture to another, so that, for example, prejudice against the French changes if we move from Canada to

Algeria (Moghaddam, 2002). In 1977 an experiment was conducted on the **prejudices of physical appearances** (Snyder, Tanke and Bershied, 1977). The subjects under examination were led by the researchers to believe, by using false photographs, that the person they were talking to on the phone was an attractive or unattractive woman. This early representation triggered different behaviors in the speaker; the style of interaction with the attractive women was judged as being friendlier, more sociable and more enjoyable than that with the unattractive women.

During an **experiment** (Tajfel & Wilkes, 1963), participants were asked to estimate the length of eight lines, which in reality, differed according to a constant ratio. For participants in Condition 1, the four shortest lines were labeled A, and the four longest lines, B. For the participants in Condition 2, the eight lines were shown without any labelling. After a series of presentations, the participants in Condition 1 showed the systematic tendency to exaggerate the differences between the lines of groups A and B and also to see the lines within each category as more similar in length than they actually were. This effect of **differentiation between groups** and **uniformity within the group** did not appear in the estimates made by the participants placed in the other two conditions.

You will wonder what the estimate of the length of some lines has to do with prejudice. It has quite a lot, to do with it, because the same fundamental consequences of categorization could be present in the **categorization of people**. Research on how individuals perceive members of internal groups as opposed to members of external groups provides data that support this view (Judd & Park, 1988). It seems that most individuals perceive more variety in their own group (<< We are different individuals with our peculiar personalities >>) than in external groups (<< They all seem the same, I really can't distinguish them >>). One of the practical consequences of this perceptual distortion is that, in legal proceedings, witnesses are more accurate in identifying members of their own ethnic group than members of other ethnic groups (Anthony, Copper and Mullen, 1992).

*Do not judge and you will
never be mistaken.*

Jean Jacques Rousseau

Small is the number of people
who see with their eyes
and think with their minds.

Albert Einstein

4

PREJUDICE AS AN INTERGROUP PROCESS

Prejudice is a subject that has aroused great interest in human and social sciences, since it refers to environments and problems - such as the relationship with diversity, discrimination, civil human society, peace, cross-cultures - of extreme theoretical, practical and political relevance. This interest has intensified since the Second World War, in relation to the discriminatory programs that developed around totalitarian ideologies, to the important forms of racism that have affected the United States of America and in recent times due to the important migration phenomenon in Europe.

Eminent Academics have indicated some personal characteristics as the **basis of prejudice**, reducing it to an **essentially individual phenomenon**, although influenced by social processes such as family education (Adorno, Frenkel - Brunswick, Levinson and Sandford, 1950).

The psycho-social perspective, on the other hand, has its own characteristic in understanding prejudice as an intergroup process (Brown, 1995). In psychosocial tradition, in fact, it is possible to find approaches and theories that, despite having different reasoning, explain prejudice and discrimination as phenomena linked to group dynamics.

Starting from Allport's (1954) now classic work, a broad consensus has been created among academics on the assumption that there is always a social categorization at the basis of prejudice: **prejudice is such because it is endured by an individual who is a member of a specific category.** In the well-known studies conducted on minimal intergroup situations, Tajfel and his colleagues (1971) found evidence to support the thesis that categorization into different groups (in group vs. out group) is a necessary and sufficient condition for the development of intergroup conflict and it is the base for discrimination of outgroup members. **The Social Identity Theory** (Tajfel and Turner, 1979) states that favoritism for the in group and discrimination of the outgroup are based on the individual motivation to maintain a high level of self-esteem: since the image of oneself is strongly linked to groups that the subject identifies himself with, he will engage in a series of social comparisons in which he will tend to promote a positive image of his own groups at the expense of the unknown groups.

On the other hand, it has been widely demonstrated that, beyond mere categorization, there are several factors that can influence the intergroup conflict (Rubini and Moscatelli, 2004). In the Sherif model (1967), **the compatibility of objectives** that the groups set themselves is a fundamental factor in the genesis of intergroup conflict. In fact, according to the author, sharing an objective is the basis of the interdependence between the members of the in group and the cooperation inside it; in the same way, the fact that in group and out group have incompatible purposes generates a situation of negative interdependence between the two groups that determines the conflict. In other words, the conflict between groups is determined by competition deriving from irreconcilable objectives and/or scarcity of resources.

This model, known as the **Theory of Realistic Conflict** (Campbell, 1965; Sherif, 1967) has been questioned by the studies of Tajfel and his collaborators; nevertheless, Tajfel himself (1982) recognized the important role that interdependence, on an objective/instrumental basis plays in intergroup conflicts, laying the foundations for prejudice and discrimination. Even in the recent international literature, there are several confirmations of the negative effect that competition on real/material bases exerts on intergroup attitudes (Esses, Dovidio, Jackson and Armstrong, 2001; Moghaddam, 2008), and extremely important topics emerge as the complex interactions between competition, cooperation, superordinate identity and perception of similarity with the outgroup (Brewer, 2005; Riketta and Sacramento, 2008).

*Listening without prejudice
or distraction is the greatest value
you can pay another person.*

Denis Waitley

*People always judge others
using the model of their own limitations
and at times the opinion of the community
is full of prejudice and fears.*

Paulo Coelho

5

NEW FORMS OF PREJUDICE

In psychosocial literature, in the last few decades, academic's have focused on "new" types of prejudice, that is, on indirect and less evident expressions of the discrimination of the outgroup that remain in the modern world, despite the widespread social regulation that makes the expression of prejudice against minorities undesirable (Pettigrew and Meertens, 1995). Therefore, alongside the " old fashioned" forms of prejudice, theoretical meanings have been proposed that refer to more subtle and less socially undesirable forms of prejudice: modern racism (Akrami, Ekehammar and Araya, 2000, McConahay, 1986), modern sexism (Benokraitis and Feagin, 1986), "aversive" racism (Gaertner and Dovidio, 1986), subtle prejudice (Pettigrew and Meertens, 1995), symbolic racism (Sears, 1988). Parallel to the effort of theoretical conceptualization, academics have pursued a methodological study that has permitted new developments with respect to the measurement of different forms of prejudice: currently a wide set of techniques is available that are differently subject to the intentional control of people, and therefore to the **influence of social desirability** (Maass, Castelli, Arcuri, 2005), ranging from the traditional pencil and paper questionnaire to the registration of physiological indexes such as skin conductance (La Barbera, Andrighetto and Trifiletti, 2007).

Between these two extremes we find some measures that allow the subjects to only have a "certain" degree of intentional control; these techniques have had a rapid success thanks to their ability to combine the merits of structured self-report tools (less intrusive, high efficiency in terms of cost-contact) with a level of measurement and representation of the phenomenon which is more refined and complex compared to more traditional instruments such as the "paper and pencil".

Among these tools is Pettigrew and Meertens's (1995) well-known **manifest and subtle prejudice scale**, which has given rise to an important theoretical and methodological debate (Pettigrew and Meertens, 2001, and Coenders, Scheepers, Snidermann and Verberk, 2001 Leone, Chirumbolo and Aiello, 2006, and Mancini and Carbone, 2007) and it has been used and validated in several countries (Hamberger and Hewstone, 1997; Pedersen and Walker, 1997; Rueda and Navas, 1996; Vala, Brito and Lopes, 1999).

Pettigrew and Meertens (1995) distinguish the blatant aspects of prejudice, more controllable and socially undesirable, from the subtle aspects, related to an indirect and deeper component of the rejection of the outgroup.

In the authors theoretic-methodological proposal, **manifest prejudice** has two components, **the perceived threat** from the outgroup and the **refusal of intimacy** with the members of the latter, while **subtle prejudice** consists of three components, **defending values and ingroup traditions**, the in group-out group **exasperation of differences** and finally **the elimination of positive emotions** towards the members of the foreign group. The two Academics have built and validated a questionnaire based on a large European sample, in order to measure the two forms of prejudice; it consists of 20 items (10 of manifest prejudice and 10 of subtle prejudice) and people are asked to indicate to what degree they agree with each item using of a 4-step scale similar to Likert's. Pettigrew and Meertens' scales have been translated and validated in Italian by

Arcuri and Boca (1996) and used in numerous studies about prejudice towards different target groups.

*Conflict is an integral part
of human life that is
within us and around us.*

Sun Tzu

*The greatest conflicts
are not between two people
but between one person and himself.*

Troyal Garth Brooks

6

THE CONFLICT

The **Allport Contact Hypothesis** (1954): To reduce the intergroup tension a number of conditions must be met:

- Equal status between the two groups in contact

If the situation is not balanced and one of the groups is in a lower position, it is probable that the current stereotypes will be strengthened.

- Successful cooperation/experience

The two groups must cooperate to achieve a common objective. If people depend on each other to obtain an objective, they have instrumental reasons for developing more friendly relationships.

- Rapporti personali e approfonditi

In depth knowledge on a personal level, which can lead to the falsification of some of the out -group's negative stereotypes due to new information. It does not necessarily lead to a perception of greater similarity.

- Institutional and social support

There are two points, the first, is a direct intervention by the authority and the possibility of sanctions in case of incorrect relations between groups or episodes of discrimination. The other point is that contact experiences cannot be isolated or limited to a single context (school, work, home...) because they would be lived as exceptions to the rule of separation between the groups.

During a study, Sherif and his colleagues made sure that two groups of students, who where rivals, cooperated in the pursuit of given objectives, that is, goals that had a strong appeal to both groups, but impossible to reach without everyone involved in a joint commitment. Problematic situations were especially created, where the two groups had to cooperate and gradually they both realized the mutual beliefs regarding the other group were false. The researchers had the definite confirmation of the solution of the conflict when the members of the two groups spent one evening happily singing and playing music all together. This experiment allowed Sherif to formulate the Theory of Realistic Conflict (Sherif, 1966).

Hostility between groups is determined by the competition for possession of material resources. The existence of opposing interests gives rise to a series of changes in the intergroup relationship for which individuals begin to think in a stereotypical way and to feed attitudes of prejudice towards the outgroup. Other research confirms this hypothesis (Haslam et al., 1992; Taylor and Moriarty, 1987).

One wonders if the simple **group membership** could influence attitudes and behavior towards individuals who are not part of it. In regards to this Tajfel developed a model called **"Minimal Group Paradigm".** In his experiments, in order to identify the minimal conditions that give rise to phenomena of discrimination towards an out-group, "groups" were created without an internal structure.

During a study (Tajfel, Billing, Bundy, Flament., 1971) the subjects believed they had to take part in a decision-making experiment. Their first task was to express an opinion of appreciation on a series of paintings by two artists. Then they were told that on the basis of their preferences they would be divided into two groups. They did not know the identity of their companions or of the members of the other group. The subjects had the task of deciding how to distribute small amounts of money among all the participants, excluding themselves. As it was a "minimal" situation, it was expected that the subjects would have assigned more or less equivalent rewards to the members of the two groups, instead the subjects tended to favor the members of their own group. This happened even at the cost of giving up the maximum profit of the in-group.

Why was there favoritism for the in-group? According to Tajfel and Turner's **Theory of Social Identity** (1979) a necessary but not sufficient condition for the behavior of the favoritism towards the in-group, is categorization. The theory of social identity emphasizes how each of us tends to look for elements that positively differentiate our membership group.

The Theory of Relative Deprivation (Davis, 1959): It is the comparison with an external group which is considered better, that leads to a state of relative deprivation, that is to a dissatisfaction with the current living conditions (Runciman,

1966). Some prerequisites that lead to the state of relative deprivation:

- The out-group must be similar to the in-group and have some desirable features

- This characteristic must also be considered pertinent to one's own group

- The absence of the desired characteristic must be considered attributable to factors   that are external to the group and not the group's fault

Social class, is a prominent feature of **intergroup conflict**, by giving less relevance to social class, stereotypes and prejudices are reduced. This is what is proposed by Brewer and Miller (1984) with the "**Model of de-categorization**" a contact, with the out-group repeated over time, that should lead to the falsification of negative beliefs associated with them. If an intergroup relationship, based on mutual tolerance, wants to be reached, it needs to be re-categorized. Another system that aims to resolve the intergroup conflict is based on **cooperation** for the achievement of given objectives. One of the most famous applications of the strategy of superordinate objectives is known as the **"The Jigsaw classroom"** (Aronson et al

1978, Aronson and Bridgeman, 1979) and is aimed at reducing the existing antagonism between classmates belonging to different races and ethnic groups.

Fig.2 *The Intergroup Contact (Zeloni Magelli, 2010)*

Without conflict, no progress,
that is the law which civilization
has followed to the present day

Karl Marx

We are always a foreigner
to someone else.
Learning how to live together
is how we fight racism.

Tahar Ben Jelloun

7

THE INTERGROUP CONTACT

According to the Contact Hypothesis (Allport, 1954), the meeting between members of different groups that occurs under favorable conditions can reduce prejudice. In the last 20 years, some theoretic models, which originate from the theory of social identity (Tajfel, 1981), have proposed to extend the hypothesis of contact in particular to identify the conditions that lead to the generalization of the positive effects of contact from known outgroup members (proximal outgroup) to un-known outgroup members (distal outgroup).

According to the **intergroup contact theory** (Brown & Hewstone, 2005), generalization is possible if, during contact, the salience of the original identities is preserved. According to the **model of the identity of the common ingroup** (Gaertner & Dovidio, 2000), the importance in the contact of a superordinate identity, which includes both the members of the in-group and those of the outgroup, can facilitate the reduction of prejudice.

Contact between members of different groups, however, can also have negative consequences, such as anxiety and uncertainty (Stephan & Stephan, 1985). Richeson and Shelton (2003, see also Richeson Trawalter, & Shelton, 2005) have shown that intergroup contact can negatively affect cognitive performance. In a series of studies, Richeson and co-workers showed that the **performance in a cognitive task** (Stroop Test) was worse for those who had contact with a member of the outgroup, compared to those who met a member of the in-group. Furthermore, this effect was present only in participants with high levels of explicit or implicit prejudice.

Research and the contact theory in the intergroup have received renewed interest in recent years. There is a constant need to **specify the processes of the intergroup contact** that explains its many effects. This is a call for continuous efforts to determine the many mediators and moderators that are involved. Greater attention is required towards negative contact. The interaction between the cross-group leading to an increase of prejudice has not been systematically studied. Rather than a situational phenomenon, contact needs to be placed in a social, multilevel, and longitudinal context. More direct applications to social policy are needed, in which contact is considered within specific institutional settings.

Ethnic prejudice can sometimes be reinforced by contact. The dominant group may feel threatened by the minority group that "occupies" spaces and resources (eg take jobs, social housing, etc.). The importance of the emotions experienced (eg irritation if the proximity is greater) is the problem of the generalization of the effect (eg I like my friend Jamal, although he is Moroccan he is really nice, but the others...).

You have a more interesting
life if you wear impressive clothes.

Vivienne Westwood

We just need
the silence of a pause,
of an amnesty:
time to reconnect
with our real identity.

Christiane Singer

8

RECENT PSYCOSOCIAL MODELS

The most recent models offered to improve intergroup relationships are based on the induction of changes in how people use social categorizations and these are *de-categorizing, re-categorizing* and *mutual differentiation*.

De-categorizing

Proposes that if the membership of a group loses priority over the consideration of another, in favor of personalized contact, then an interpersonal meeting, rather than intergroup meeting, is possible: this should facilitate the reduction of favoritism towards one's own group (Brewer and Miller ,1984). One of the problems with this approach is the difficulty of generalization, from the interpersonal meeting with that person or those people to the improvement of the attitude towards the whole group of ethnic minority.

Re-categorizing

It aims to structure group classification at a higher and more inclusive level. It is achieved by increasing the importance of cross-group or superordinate group memberships, encouraging the fact that people perceive others as a members of a group close to their own on a given dimension, improving, in this way, the intergroup relationships. An example is the introduction of a common in-group identity (Gaertner and Dovidio, Anastasio, Bachman and Rust, 1993), transforming the representation of belonging to two groups into one single inclusive group. (Eg yes, we are white and black but we are all students from the same school).

Mutual differentiation

It encourages groups to emphasize their distinctiveness but in a context of cooperative interconnection. It is basically a matter of safeguarding the differences between groups/cultures (where minorities often feel threatened in their specific attempts of integration) while emphasizing that the meetings take place with typical members of a group and not with unusual members, i.e., individuals who may be nice but that don't represent the ethnic group at all. This should allow the modification of stereotypes and the generalization of positive attitudes towards the entire outgroup (Hewstone & Brown, 1986).

*People have prejudices about nations
that they know nothing about.*

Philip Gilbert Hamerton

*My hope for the planet lies
in my children and grandchildren.*

Joanne Woodward

9

FUTURE DIRECTIONS FOR THE THEORY OF CONTACT IN THE INTERGROUP

In literature, hundreds of essays and chapters have been written about intergroup contact during the last few decades. This intense renewed interest in Allport's (1954) simple theory has led to an emerging area of the social psychology of intergroup relations. The hypothesis has spread into a developed theory (Brown & Hewston, 2005; Pettigrew, 1998) and shows that it is applicable to a wide variety of groups and categories. His main argument is that contact typically reduces **prejudice in the intergroup** and this has received a solid meta-analytical support. A meta-analysis of 516 studies obtained an average measurement of effect between contact and prejudice of $r = -0.21$. It also turned out that 95% of the 516 studies report a negative correlation between contact and prejudice of many types. But there is diversification in the measurement of prejudice, detecting wider effects of cognitive indicators and stereotypes. A more rigorous and recent research with experimental studies produced a higher average, with a result of an effect of $r = -0.33$. These results and their implications began a focused effort to understand the process and **maximize its effect**.

As we saw before, the Allport contact theory (1954) declares that the following conditions must be met to reduce intergroup tensions:

- **equal status between the two groups in contact**

- **successful cooperation/experience**

- **personal and in-depth relationships**

- **institutional and social support**

The meta-analytical examination indicates, however, that these conditions offer a package that facilitates the effect, but it is not essential to reduce prejudice (Pettigrew & Tropp, 2006). Friendship in the cross-group is likely to embrace many of Allport's conditions. These friendships can provide extensive contact in multiple social contexts with access to cross-group friendship networks and opportunities for self-disclosure. In fact, research has repeatedly confirmed that friendship is substantially negatively connected to prejudice. In fact, **the reduction of prejudice connected to friendship** (in the intergroup) will be applied even to the other outgroups that are not involved in the contact situation. Prejudiced people avoid contact with the objects of their prejudice and the non-prejudiced will look for such contact. Longitudinal studies of contact effects are rare. But the few that exist reveal that **optimal contact reduces prejudices** over time, even when researchers have eliminated the possibility of participant selection. Therefore, different methods converge to suggest that while both sequences operate, the most important effect is the reduction of prejudice in the intergroup contact.

With all the attention now dedicated to the subject, the contact theory is advancing rapidly in many new directions. Pettigrew & Tropp (2006) in their meta-analysis of contact found effects that the theory is equally good for groups, different ethnic groups, races and cultural groups for which the theory was originally intended. These other types are often stigmatized outgroups such as homosexuals, (Herek & Capitanio, 1996), the homeless (Lee, Farrel, and Link, 2004) and physically and mentally disabled (Pettigrew &

Tropp, 2006). Improving **the contact attitudes of the intergroup**, then, is a general phenomenon. Its relevance suggests that it could be connected to basic processes, such as **the effect of simple exposition** of Zajonc (1968). Researchers have repeatedly shown that greater exposure to targets can significantly increase the desire for that target. Works on the relationship between exposure and fondness indicates that the reduction of uncertainty is an important mechanism underlying these relationships (Lee, 2001). Stephan, Stephan and Gudykunst (1999) began the task of combining the reduction of uncertainty and threat reduction theories.

To complete this vision, remarkable recent research aims to the importance of this reduction of threat in the intergroup and to reducing anxiety to achieve **reductions of prejudice**. The psychological researches of Blascovich, Mendes, Hunter and Lickel (2000) and Mendes, Blascovich, Lickel and Hunter (2002) are impressive. These researchers note that American college students who have had extensive experience with African Americans show significantly less anxiety about the interaction between groups, compared to students without such experiences. The studies have also employed a wide range of dependent variables, besides just the reduction of prejudice, even if some critics of the contact theory seem to ignore this development (Dixon, Durcheim and Tredoux, 2005). This work reveals that having friends in the out-group leads to **positive effects** which go beyond the simple reduction of prejudice. Therefore, participants in cross-group friendships generally perceive greater variability in outgroups than others. Contact can also lead to greater **empathy** with outgroups, as well as **reducing interactional anxiety**.

In fact, as written below, the reduction of anxiety and the increase of empathy could be (will be) essential mediators for other positive effects of contact. Recent research in Northern Ireland shows that friendship in the intergroup can also generate **forgiveness and trust** among Catholics and Protestants who have personally suffered from the sectarian violence of the province (Hewstone, Cairns, Voci, Hamberger and Niens, 2006). Wright, Aron, McLaughlin-Volpe and Roppe (1997) introduced another major expansion. These researchers proposed a process of extensive indirect contact. With American college students, they presented both correlational and experimental evidence to show that simply **having friends in the in-group who have friends in the outgroup** helps to decrease prejudice. This has been repeated in Europe, on two samples of

Northern Ireland. Paolini, Hewstone, Cairns and Voci (2004) have shown that **indirect contact has the power to reduce prejudice.** And the data analysis of a German report also discovered indirect contact effects. But the changed attitudes produced by indirect contact are not as strong as "direct". For example, they can easily change and return to the initial stage.

In any case, the effects of indirect contact are particularly important for those living in segregated areas who have no friends in the outgroup. The vast majority of group contact studies have focused on the effects of the majority or a more powerful and non-stigmatized group in interaction. Recently however, a series of studies by Richeson and Shelton (2007) focused on the minority. They show that African-American students who expect white people to be influenced by prejudice, and those who had negative attitudes about white people, report many negative experiences in **interracial contact** (Shelton & Richeson, 2006). At least in the meetings, the black participants liked the white participants who did their best to be less biased even though they probably were more so (Shelton, Richeson and Salvatore, 2005, Shelton, Richeson, Salvatore and Trawalter, 2005). This research, combined with other work (for example, Chavous,

2005; Richeson & Shelton 2007; Tropp, 2003) highlights the important point **that contact theory must take into account the subjective factors of both the majority and minority members.**

This recent progress raises new questions and increases the prospect of future developments. Among the many possibilities four interconnected directions seem current and probable:

- *Specify the processes of contact*

- *Greater attention to contact that leads to negative effects: increase in prejudice, mistrust and conflict*

- *Position the contact in its social, longitudinal and multi-level context*

- *Apply the contact to a multi-level social policy*

9.1

SPECIFY THE PROCESSES OF THE CONTACT

Today we know a lot about how the majorities and the minorities see and react to intergroup contact. Now these rival perspectives must be combined into one dynamic multi-level model. A beginning towards this ambitious goal is a clearer and more detailed description of the effects of contact mediators. With 63 studies and 81 independent samples that have studied the effects on prejudice, Pettigrow & Tropp (in press) conducted a series of meta-analyzes to verify the importance of the three most widespread mediators studied: *a new knowledge of the outgroup, the reduction of anxiety* and *empathy with the outgroup.*

The first contact theorists thought that knowledge of contact reduced prejudice. Recent studies, however, have revealed that the mediation of knowledge exists, but it is of minor importance.

Empathy and *perspective taking* are much more important. Contacts in the cross-group and above all friendship, allow one to **be attuned** and **understand the point of view of the outgroup**. This research is based on the work of Batson, Lishner, Cook and Sawyer (2005). This is also relevant in McFarland's studies (1999), with samples of students and adults; Empathy is an important mediator related to prejudice along with authoritarianism and the orientation of social dominance.

In a similar way Vescio, Sechrist and Paolucci (2003) found that **the conquest of perspective**, in an experimental environment, led to a more favorable racial point of view. The reduction of intergroup threat and anxiety is also critical (Blascovich, Mendes, Hunter, Lickel, & Kowai-Bell, 2001; Islam & Hewstone, 1993; Paolini et al., 2004; Pettigrew, 1998; Stephan et al., 2002; Voci & Hewstone, 2003). Anxiety springs from feelings of threat and uncertainty that people experience in intergroup contexts. These feelings arise from concerns about how we should act, how we are perceived and how and if we are accepted (Richeson & Shelton, 2007). It is noted that emotional mediators (empathy and anxiety reduction) are more important than cognitive ones (knowledge), even though both play an important role. Let's remember that Tropp and Pettigrew (2005a) have found that prejudice is reduced more by **affective components** than cognitive ones. Research needs to develop this area further.

9.2

A GREATER ATTENTION TO CONTACT THAT LEADS TO NEGATIVE EFFECTS: AN INCREASE OF PREJUDICE, MISTRUST AND CONFLICT

In their study carried out on 713 independent samples of contact during the twentieth century, Pettigrew and Tropp found only a 34% (<5%) of positive relationships between contact groups that improved prejudice. There are still negative results in dangerous situations and research must dedicate more attention to this. When Williams (1947) and Allport (1954) were forming the contact theory, they assumed that **too much contact did not reduce prejudice.** They therefore tried to specify the positive traits in those situations that could maximize the potential for contact to promote a positive intergroup relationship. But meta-analytic results reveal that our understanding of contact is limited by this emphasis on positive contact.

There are negative factors such as anxiety, authoritarianism and regulatory restrictions that deserve more attention because they can become key points for future research of intergroup contact. Such emphasis would allow a more complete understanding of the conditions that increase and inhibit the potential positive effects of contact. Here are the first results of the analysis conducted using two means of positive and negative contact with foreigners residing in Germany. The two types of contact are compared with the data obtained from a 2004 telephone survey carried out on 1383 German citizens aged 16 and above who do not have an immigration background.

This survey, which is part of a extensive, 10-year project on prejudice, conducted by Heitmeyer (2004) of the University of Bielefeld, offers a wide range of indicators of great relevance both for the contact among groups and for prejudice. These foreign residents began arriving in Germany in the 50s; many are second and third generation, but very few have been able to become German citizens.

Even though they come from many countries, the prototype consists of Turkish-Muslim immigrants. In fact, *the anti-Muslim measure correlates highly to a measure of anti-foreign prejudice* (r = +0.65). Obviously, there are enormous differences between the two cultures.

These are the items used for the various measures analyzed (Sidanius & Pratto, 1999) and (Altemeyer, 1996):

Inter-group positive contact (alpha= 0.78)

1. How often has a foreigner helped you? Often, sometimes, rarely or never?

2. How often do you have an interesting conversation with a foreigner? Often, sometimes, rarely or never?

3. and **4.** Now think about meetings with foreigners in Germany. How often have you experienced the following feelings *(3)* satisfied and *(4)* cheerful? - never, sometimes, often or very often?

Negative contact of the intergroup (alpha= 0.78)

1. How often has a foreigner bothered you? Never, sometimes, often or very often?

2-4. Think now about meetings with foreigners in

Germany. How often have you experienced the following feelings *(2)* anger *(3)*, irritation and *(4)* fear - never, sometimes, often or very often?

Three conditions of contact:

1. How would you judge your contacts with foreigners living here in Germany - superficial, on equal terms and voluntary? It does not apply at all, it tends not to apply, it tends to apply, it fully applies

Individual threat (r= 0.68):

1. Foreigners living here are a threat to my personal freedom and to my rights. - It does not apply at all, it tends not to apply, it tends to apply, it fully applies.

2. Foreigners living here are a threat to my personal economic situation. - It does not apply at all, it tends not to apply, it tends to apply, it fully applies.

Group threat (r= 0.67):

1. Foreigners living here are a threat to our personal freedom and rights. - It does not apply at all, it tends not to apply, it tends to apply, it fully applies.

2. Foreigners living here are a threat to our economic well-being. - It does not apply at all, it tends not to apply, it tends to apply, it fully applies.

Political conservativism:

1. Thinking about your political vision, would you classify yourself as left winged, fairly left winged, in the center, fairly right winged, right winged?

Scale of social domain (alpha= 0.61):

1. Groups on the bottom of our society should stay there - I completely disagree, I tend to disagree, I tend to agree, I totally agree.

2. Some groups of populations are more useful than others – I completely disagree, I tend to disagree, I tend to agree, I completely agree.

3. Some groups are worth less than others - I completely disagree, I tend to disagree, I tend to agree, I totally agree.

Scale of authoritarianism (alpha= 0.75):

1. Crime should be punished very severely - I completely disagree, I tend to disagree, I tend to agree, I totally agree.

2. To ensure law and order, one should act more severely towards outsiders and those who create problems — I completely disagree, I tend to disagree, I tend to agree, I completely agree.

3. Two of the most important characteristics should be obedience and respect towards superiors - I completely disagree, I tend to disagree, I tend to agree, I completely agree.

Anti-Muslim prejudice (alpha= 0.75):

1. The Muslim culture fits well in our Western world - I totally agree, I tend to agree, I tend to disagree, I completely disagree.

2. With many Muslims living in Germany, I sometimes feel like a foreigner in my own country - I completely disagree, I tend to disagree, I tend to agree, I completely agree.

3. Muslim migration should be forbidden - I completely disagree, I tend to disagree, I tend to agree, I totally agree.

4. I am more suspicious of Muslims - I completely disagree, I tend to disagree, I tend to agree, I totally agree.

5. The many mosques in Germany prove that Islam wants to expand its power – I completely disagree, I tend to disagree, I tend to agree, I completely agree.

As indicated by these items, we have four questions that take advantage of the positive contact (alpha = 0.78). Another four, take advantage of the negative contact (alpha = 0.78). Furthermore, the survey asked participants to evaluate three conditions of their contact: whether it was superficial, on an equal basis, or voluntary.

The survey also assessed the possibility of the participants feeling threatened by foreign residents on both a personal and group level. We have seen the two items used to calculate the personal threat (r = 0.68), and the two parallel items used to calculate the group threat (r = 0.67). The single item on political conservatism has also been shown. The three items took advantage of the orientation of social dominance (alpha = 0.61) and authoritarianism (alpha = 0.75). Lastly, the last five items calculated the prejudice of the interviewees (alpha = 0.78).

The results with the two contact measurements suggest that **positive and negative contact have different dynamics.** However, they are clearly not polar-opposite phenomena. First of all, the positive and negative contact measurements were related only to - 0.18 (p <0.01). The ratio is retained by participants who had a considerable positive and slightly negative intergroup contact.

Predictors of positive and negative contact

Predictor variables	Positive contact			Negative Contact		
	St. Beta	t	p	St. Beta	t	p
Authoritarianism	-0.068	**-2.19**	**0.03**	-0.034	-1.14	0.25
Social dominance	-0.012	-0.42	0.68	0.027	0.92	0.36
Political conservatism	-0.054	**-1.94**	**0.052**	0.044	1.63	0.10
Age	-0.029	-1.09	0.28	-0.221	**-8.41**	**0.001**
Individual threat	-0.151	**-4.65**	**0.001**	0.312	**9.84**	**0.001**
Collective threat	-0.119	**-3.41**	**0.001**	0.181	**5.35**	**0.001**
Non-superficial contact	0.194	**7.07**	**0.001**	0.012	0.46	0.64
Equal Status contact	0.207	**7.60**	**0.001**	-0.012	-0.46	0.65
Voluntary contact	0.085	**2.97**	**0.003**	-0.138	**-4.99**	**0.001**
R^2	0.52			0.56		
N	1085			1093		

Bold indicates statistically significant results that are described in text.

Tabella 1 Prediction of positive and negative contact (Pettigrow, 2008)

Secondly, as measured by the scales the positive contact ($r = -0.41$) is more predictive of the anti-Muslim prejudice than the negative ($r = +0.30$). Using Blalock's formula (1972) to compare correlations within the same sample, this difference is highly significant ($t = 22.2$, $p < 0.001$).

Thirdly, different types of people tend to be involved in the two different types of contact. The participants who were not very authoritative, who are neither threatened by immigrants, nor politically conservative, are more likely to report a positive contact. In contrast, those who reported negative contact are younger and feel threatened by immigrants, both individually and collectively. It is interesting to note that the position of social dominance does not contribute to the prediction of gender or education.

Fourthly, the social contexts of the two phenomena differ significantly. Positive contact occurs at work ($r = +0.28$, $p < 0.001$) and especially in the neighborhood ($r = +0.36$, $p < 0.001$). Negative contact is not connected to contact with the neighborhood ($r = -0.02$, n.s.) and only slightly connected to contact at work ($r = +0.13$, $p < 0.01$) where job competition could exist. The table also shows that both types of contact are conditioned by contexts of situations reported by the participants, as Allport (1954) claimed in his original hypothesis. Positive contact is significantly and relatively connected to all three conditions - *not superficial*, on an *equal status* and *voluntary*. In fact, these three conditions significantly relate to the negative relationship between positive contact and anti-Muslim attitude. That is, each of these conditions helps to explain the link of positive contact with reduced anti-Muslim attitudes: *not superficial* (Sobel test = -0.03, p <0.003), *equal status* (Sobel test = -4.06, p <0.0001) and *voluntary contact* (Sobel test = -4.47, p <0.0001) (Sobel's test provides the critical report).

However, all three conditions also relate to the link between negative contact and increase of prejudice: *non-superficial* (Sobel test = 3.10, p <0.002), *equal status* (Sobel test = 3.83, p <0.0002) and *voluntary contact* (Sobel test = 4.2, p <0.0001). Only the ratio of exposed moderators implies an equal status.

The association between the moderators of negative contact and prejudice is significant (interaction t = 3.68, p <0.001). Thus, for the situations judged by the participants as not being of equal status, the correlation of negative contact with anti-Muslim opinions is only +0.13; but when they are judged to be of equal status, the correlation rises to +0.36. This interaction coincides with Table 1 and is the demonstration of the **importance of threat** in links between prejudice and both positive and negative contact; a point underlined by Stephan and Stephan (1985). For both collective and personal threat, positive contact is associated with a reduced threat, and negative contact with a greater threat.

These results are consistent with our previous discussion on the importance of **interactional anxiety.** All in all, the distribution of the answers on the two scales differ clearly. This random sample of German participants reports a relationship which is much more positive than negative (t = 36.2, p <0.0001). Therefore 85% of the participants said they had interesting conversations with foreign citizens and 63% reported having been helped sometimes by foreigners. 65% of respondents report never having been bothered by foreigners. Part of this difference could be related to **"social desirability",** but the consistency of the results with the positive and negative contact measurements suggests that this possible effect is rare. These strong differences between the two groups of interactions are both of theoretical and political importance. Remember that these differences emerge from a probabilistic sample of a German non-immigrant population. Because negative contacts are often advertised, while positive ones are either not acknowledged nor generate any news, these results may seem surprising. However, the prelevance of positive intergroup contact helps to explain why the contact that leads to an increase in injury is so relatively rare in research literature.

9.3

POSITION THE CONTACT OF THE INTERGROUP IN A SOCIAL, LONGITUDINAL AND MULTI-LEVEL CONTEXT

We have noticed that research literature on contact suffers from a lack of both longitudinal and multi-level studies. The meta-analysis of Pettigrow and Tropp (2006), after analyzing the research data of the twentieth century, discovered that only two longitudinal studies had been carried out and no multi-level studies carried out. A brilliant study on the field by Sherif (1966), Robbers' cave, offered the first almost-experimental field study with positive results for the contact theory. The critical point of Sherif 's famous research study was that he obtained repeated attitude measures while contact experiences developed among his two groups of young boys (Pettigrew 1991). More recently, several longitudinal studies have been published that support the theory (Eller & Abrams 2003/2004).

The research performed with a five-point data collection over a 4-year period with more than 2,000 university students at the University of California in Los Angeles, is particularly impressive (Levin et al., 2003). The study also boasts an almost-experimental design randomly assigning roommates of different ethnic groups. This extensive work provides a model for future research that examines collective effects with extraordinary data within a particular institutional setting.

These researchers have found significant mutual effects over the years: **inter-ethnic friendships** reduced prejudice, while the initial ingroup-bias and the intergroup anxiety led to a lower quantity of friends in the intergroup. These are the non-recurring effects between the intergroup contact and prejudice that have been consistently found everywhere in contact research literature. However, researchers of U.C.L.A. found that the path from prejudice to reduced contact and friendship could be stronger than in the previous research. Two sets of the U.C.L.A results are particularly important. In the first place, randomly assigned roommates of different ethnic groups reduced their prejudices on outgroups even for outgroups not involved in rooming relationships. This wide **generalization effect** was previously discovered only in uncontrolled research data (Pettigrew, 1997). Secondly, from a multilevel perspective, the ingroup organizations of the U.C.L.A. campus usually had negative individual effects. Group memberships such as fraternities strengthened contact with the ingroup and a sense of ethnic victimization while contact with the outgroup decreased. After checking the attitudes of the students before they went to university, the researchers of U.C.L.A. discovered that fraternity and participation to women's associations significantly increased opposition to greater diversity on the campus and to interethnic meetings and marriages. This organized membership was also associated with a higher score on a symbolic measure of racism.

Another way of looking at the evolving development of intergroup contact in its social context is to think in terms of a set of **collective random processes** including a series of phases of selection. Although it is best studied through longitudinal data, the point can be illustrated with data from the research survey used previously (Heitmeyer, 2004).

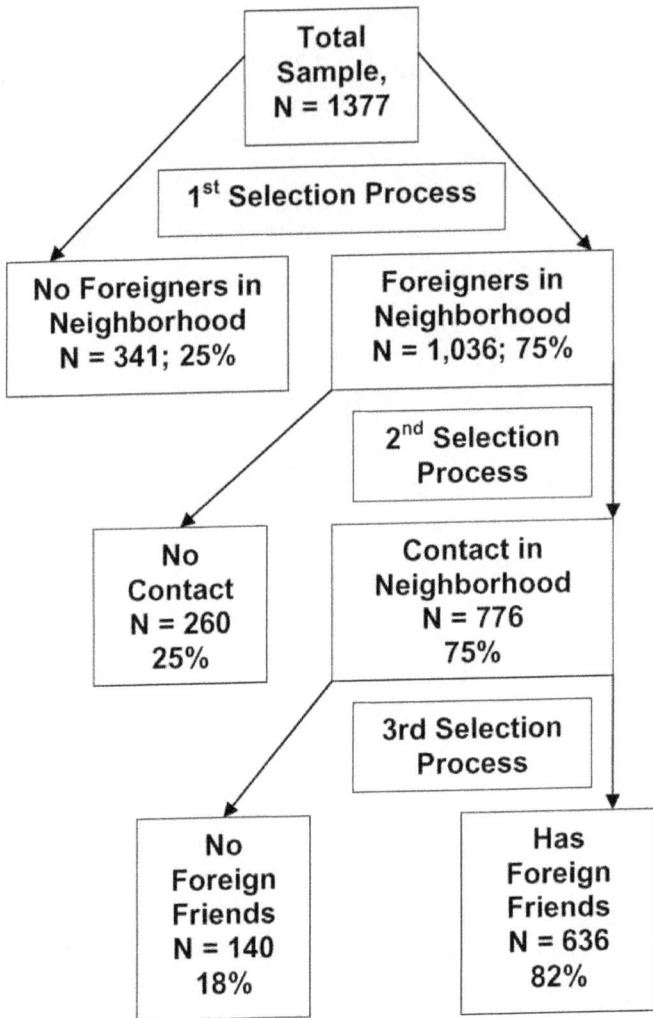

Fig. 3 three selection processes (Pettirgew, 2008)

Figure 3 illustrates a model that uses **3 separate processes connected to neighborhood contact.** The first selection process includes Germans living in neighborhoods with foreign residents, obviously an indispensable requirement for contact. Figure 3 shows that its selection eliminates 25% of the total sample. But the mere presence of foreigners does not guarantee contact with the intergroup; the second selection process. In fact, 25% of interviewed Germans living in mixed areas declare that they have don't have any contact with foreigners. Finally, simple contact does not guarantee that friendship within the intergroup will develop. Interestingly, this last selection process eliminates only 18% of those interviewed who have contact with neighbors.

Table 2 tests the predictors of these three selection processes. **Education**, surprisingly, does not emerge as a significant correlation in any of the three selections, but two social variables are important. **Age** proves to be significant on two points; the youngest participants are more likely to live in a mixed neighborhood and make friends after contact with foreigners in the neighborhood.

Gender becomes more important in the last two phases of selection; males have more contact with foreign neighbors and have more friends. This result reflects the fact that foreign men are more likely to learn the German language and culture than women; this is because they are more likely to be in the workforce.

Two psychological variables are also implied in these processes. **Authoritarianism** is highly negatively correlated to all three processes.

Authoritarians are less likely to live in an area with foreigners and are less likely to have contact with them even when they live in these areas and they are less likely to make friends even with those who have foreign friends. In other analyses, positive authoritarianism has been shown to be a strong negative mediator of intergroup contact. The available data indicates that this mediation consists of authoritarians who generally make sure they avoid foreign residents at multiple levels.

Predictors of the three selection processes

Predictor variables	Are there foreign neighbors? 1st selection process			Contact with foreign neighbors? 2nd selection process			Any foreign friends? 3rd selection process		
	St. Beta	t	p	St. Beta	t	p	St. Beta	t	p
Respondent's age	-0.111	-4.10	0.001	0.026	0.83	0.406	-0.111	-3.22	0.001
Respondent's gender	0.007	0.27	0.784	-0.087	-2.81	0.005	-0.072	-2.08	0.038
Authoritarianism	-0.111	-3.63	0.001	-0.088	-2.49	0.013	-0.096	-2.46	0.014
Anti-Muslim prejudice	-0.038	-1.24	0.214	-0.084	-2.39	0.017	-0.208	-5.26	0.001
N	1377			1036			636		

Tabella 2 I predittori dei tre processi di selezione (Pettigrew, 2008)

Table 2 also shows the reverse sequence in the causal **contact-prejudice** link that was often found in previous studies. The people interviewed, who are highly prejudiced against Muslims (previous items by Sidanius & Pratto and Altemeyer) are less likely to have contact and make friends with foreign neighbors after contact (second and third phase of the selection). These results raise a further issue concerning the overall effects of the reduction of intergroup prejudice and positive contact.

Table 2 shows that seniors, women and authoritarians have reduced intergroup contact and friendship. But do these factors reduce the effects of prejudice even when friendship and other positive contacts are achieved? In other words, do these contact-limiting factors also act as moderators of the contact-prejudice relationship? For example, do authoritarians who have positive contacts, also have a reduced anti-Muslim attitude?

The answer from this data is no. Despite the age (interaction $t = 0.51$, ns), sex (interaction $t = 0.39$, ns) and authoritarianism (interaction $t = -1.41$, ns) all limit the contact, they do not influence the power of positive contact to reduce the prejudice until the purpose has been reached.

For example, the correlation between positive contact and anti-Muslim prejudice is -0.36 among those who have a low level of authoritarianism and -0.39 among those with a high level of authoritarianism. The same lack of moderation of age (interaction t = 0.40), sex (interaction t = 0.27) and education (interaction t = 1.69, p <0.10) also exists for negative contact. This placement of intergroup contact, in its evolving social context, has direct implications on politics.

Social policy can facilitate such contact even for those who otherwise try to avoid it. And the results of table 2 suggest that such contact, although it is involuntary, will have beneficial effects in the intergroup.

9.4

APPLY INTERGROUP CONTACT TO MULTI-LEVEL SOCIAL POLICY

A final, hoped-for direction for the future concerns the direct application to social policy of what has been comprehended about the contact of the intergroup. In Great Britain, Miles Houston used the contact theory effectively to influence government efforts **to reduce intergroup conflict** in Northern Ireland. In the United States, social psychologists have made extensive use of the theory in the testimony of the court in the courthouse and first in public interventions concerning disruption at school and the Affirmative action (Pettigrew, 1967, 1969). During these activities, contact theory led directly to a fundamental distinction that has now entered public speech in the USA.

This distinction outlines the simple disintegration, the physical mixture of groups, from the real integration-situations that approach the encounter of Allport's four key conditions of optimal contact.

Gurin, Dey, Hurtado and Gurin (2002) and Gurin, Lehman and Lewis (2004) gave a substantial contribution to two cases of action in front of the US Supreme Court. These researchers have emphasized **the beneficial effects of intergroup contact** in the education sector for both the majority and the minority of students. Their work was widely spread by the mass media and was cited in the opinions of the High Court.

But such direct applications of the theory are not universally accepted in social sciences. For example, critics of political science, such as McGarry and O'Leary (1995), declared that contact is more likely to **cause conflicts** than reduce prejudice. They also think that reducing prejudice does not necessarily lead to changes on a structural level.

These critics seem to ignore the actual claims of the theory and the massive scientific literature that supports research. "Sometimes", McGarry and O'Leary (1995) write, "good fences make good neighbors". Let's consider the repeated failures of the "good fences", from the Great Wall of China to Hadrian's Wall on the Scottish border, or the modern examples of the Berlin Wall and the West Bank Wall in Israel. From these important experiments it was rare to find "good neighbors" with "good fences". But we have to dig deeper to understand the skepticism of these two scientists. McGarry and O'Leary focus on the tragic events between Catholics and Protestants in their native Northern Ireland. They point out that contact can, under the hostile regulatory conditions that have long characterized the Ulster, currently confirm and increase prejudice rather than reduce it. Naturally, the contact theory allows these negative effects to happen to a large extent.

More fundamentally, McGarry and O'Leary criticize two major themes: the first is that contact does not necessarily reduce prejudice, at least not in Northern Ireland; the second is that, even if it did, **the reduction is irrelevant** to a wider structural policy and to the reduction of wars and conflicts.

The first statement is easily discredited by the meta-analysis described above that included studies from Northern Ireland. We have also noted that negative contact can increase prejudice. But these cases are much less common than those involving **positive contact and friendship.** Furthermore, recent studies by Irish social psychologists find that the Catholic-Protestant contact typically decreases prejudice at the same level of contact in other parts of the world. Going forward, we noticed before that even the North-Irish people interviewed who had friends of the same religion, also having friends of the other, revealed to be less bigots (Paolini, 2004). Friendship created trust and forgiveness among Catholics and Protestants who had directly suffered this kind of violence.

More important is by McGarry and O'Leary's second claim, which states that **contact is irrelevant to politics.** Note that this statement is an assertion that the micro-phenomenon (for example, prejudice of the intergroup) has little to do with the macro-phenomenon (violence and conflict). This is a recurrent debate within sociology, as well as micro-level disciplines at micro level and meso-level such as social psychology and moreover macro-level disciplines at macro level such as political science. Such statements are questionable at various levels of analysis.

It is the task of social science to put the levels together in a larger and more useful multi-level model. Some social scientists have achieved this mission and shown that it is not only possible but absolutely necessary that the results of social sciences be successfully applied to the current problems of society. For example, Kelman (in press) has shown how the use of problem-solving workshops with multiple group participants can influence national and cultural policies even in the current conflicts in the Middle East.

Intergroup contact specialists have never claimed that contact was a cure for macro-level conflicts. In fact, they explicitly rejected these statements (Hewstone, 2003). But to state that prejudice has little or nothing to do with the conflict of the intergroup is an extreme position, to say the least. Rather, many results, so far, reveal that contact is a necessary but not a sufficient condition alone to resolve the conflict of the intergroup.

A more valid criticism, however, would be that social psychologists have not yet paid enough attention to transform the contact theory into a more easily applicable remedy within specific **institutional settings**. In particular, practical applications require a structural and multi-level context for contact policies. How to structure optimal contact situations in realistic institutional locations? All three of the previous discussed directions would contribute to answers to this critical question: specifying the contact processes, a greater focus on intergroup leading to negative effects and placing contact in its longitudinal, multi-level and social context. Clearly, much remains to be done to make the theory of contact and research more easily applicable to social policy.

Experience does not err;
it is only your judgment that errs
in expecting from her
what is not in her power.

Leonardo da Vinci

Man's judgment of values
directly follows his wishes for happiness,
that they are an attempt to support
his illusions with arguments.

Sigmund Freud

10

CONTACT AND EFFECTS ON COGNITIVE FUNCTIONING AND OUTGROUP EVALUATIONS

As we have seen previously, according to the Contact Hypothesis (Allport, 1954), encounters between members of different groups, that take place under favorable conditions, can reduce prejudice. In the last 20 years, some theoretical models, which derive their origin from the theory of social identity (Tajfel, 1981), have offered to extend the hypothesis of contact in particular to identify the conditions that lead to the **generalization of the positive effects** of contact from known outgroup members (proximal outgroup) to unknown outgroup members (distal outgroups). According to the intergroup contact theory (Brown & Hewstone, 2005), generalization is possible if, during contact, **the importance of the original identities** is preserved. According to the model of the identity of the common ingroup (Gaertner & Dovidio, 2000), the importance during the contact of a superordinate identity, which includes both the members of the ingroup and those of the out-group, can facilitate a reduction in prejudice.

Contact between members of different groups can also have negative consequences, such as anxiety and uncertainty (Stephan & Stephan, 1985). Richeson and Shelton (2003, see also Richeson Trawalter, & Shelton, 2005) have shown that **intergroup contact** can negatively affect cognitive performance. In a series of studies, Richeson and his collaborators showed that performance in a cognitive task (Stroop Test) was worse for those who had contact with a member of the outgroup, compared to those who met a member of the ingroup. Furthermore, this effect was present only in participants with high levels of explicit or implicit prejudice.

60 Italian students (12 males, 48 females) from the Faculty of Psychology (The University of Padua) were examined in a study. The average age was 23.47 (standard deviation = 3.00). The experimental pattern was one-way on three levels: two-groups, one-group, control, with random allocation of the participants to the three experimental conditions. The participants were individually examined in the laboratory. The research was presented as a study on the

influence of a cognitive task on a second cognitive task, separated by a short interval. The experiment was divided into three parts.

In the first part, the participants completed the *Implicit Association Test* (IAT, Greenwald, McGhee, & Schwartz, 1998), and the scale of affective prejudice (Pettigrew & Meertens, 1995), to determine, the respective implicit and explicit attitude towards Albanians.

In the second part, the participants were taken into a second laboratory, where they had to help a second experimenter create experimental stimuli for a fake study. The task was to give a brief presentation of oneself (one minute) and to give one's opinion on two topics (the order of presentation was counterbalanced): (a) the reform of the Italian university system; (b) the arrival of illegal immigrants on the Italian coasts (two minutes for each topic). In the two contact conditions (two-groups, one-group), the second experimenter was Albanian; in the condition of control, the second experimenter was Italian. The interactions were videotaped. In the two-group condition, the experimenter apologized for his grammatical errors, due to his Albanian origin. Moreover, during the interaction, he emphasized his foreign accent and made many grammatical errors. In the one-group condition, similarly to the two-group condition, the Albanian experimenter apologized for his grammatical errors, due to his origins however he made very few mistakes. Moreover, before introducing the task to the participant, he said that he too was a student and that the study was regarding his degree thesis, thus giving importance to the common identity of the psychology students. Lastly, in the condition of control, the experimenter was Italian.

In the third part of the experiment, the participant was taken to the first laboratory where, in the presence of the first experimenter, he completed a Stroop Test and a questionnaire with explicit measures.

The tools that were used are the following:

- IAT

The IAT (Greenwald et al., 1998) measures the implicit attitudes towards social groups, establishing the strength of association between target concepts (eg, Italians vs. Albanians) and evaluation attributes (eg, positive words vs negative words). In our study, the IAT was applied using the *Inquisit* software (version 1.33; Draine, 2003). Four categories of stimuli were used, each consisting of 10 items: Italian names, Albanian names, positive words and negative words. The positive and negative words were adapted by Greenwald ,et al. (1998). The Italian names were taken from previous studies that indicated the typical characteristics of the Italian group (e.g., Capozza, Andrighetto, & Falvo, 2007); The Albanian names were selected by an Italian judge and an Albanian judge on the basis of their perceived typical characteristics. The task of the participants was to categorize the items belonging to the four categories of stimuli, which appeared one at a time in the center of the screen, as quickly as possible, using two response keys.

There were two experimental blocks. In the first, Italian names and positive words shared a key response, while the Albanian names and negative words shared another key response. In the second, the associations were inverted: Italian names and negative words shared a key response, while the other key was associated with Albanian names and positive words. The order of presentation of the response blocks was counterbalanced between the participants.

- Stroop Test

The words "red", "yellow", "blue", "green", or a row of "X's" were presented individually in the center of the screen in one of the four colors: red, yellow, green, blue. In compatible tests, each word appeared in its respective color (e.g.: "green" written in green), or the row of "X" was presented in one of the four colors. In the incompatible tests, each word was written with a different color from its semantic meaning (e.g.: "green" written in red). Each stimulus was presented for a maximum of 800 ms, preceded by a fixation point (+). The *inter-stimulus interval* was 1500 ms. The task of the participants was to indicate, as quickly as possible, the color in which a stimulus was presented by pressing one of four keys on the computer keyboard. There were seven experimental blocks, each consisting of 12 stimuli: four incompatible, eight compatible.

- Questionnaire

Control of experimental manipulation

The participants expressed their degree of agreement with the following two statements on a seven-degree scale (completely disagree - agree to the maximum degree): "During the interaction with the second experimenter " "I perceived that we belonged to a common group "; "I perceived belonging to two distinct groups".

Explicit prejudice
(measured before the manipulation)

The items of the affective injury scale were used (Pettigrew & Meertens, 1995). The participants expressed, on a five-level scale (not at all-very much), solidarity and admiration felt for Italians (alpha = .62) and for the Albanians living in Italy (alpha = .73). The index of affective prejudice was calculated by obtaining the difference between these indices: high scores express higher explicit prejudice towards the Albanians.

Negative stereotypes

The participants indicated the typical characteristic perceived, compared to the Albanian group, of three items that, during a pretest, resulted as being typical of the Albanians: aggressive, overbearing, violent. The scale had seven levels: the scores from 1 to 3 indicated decreasing degrees of typical characteristics; 4 indicated that the character was neither typical nor atypical of the Albanians; the scores from 5 to 7 indicated increasing degrees of typical characteristics. The three items were combined (alpha = .85).

Value of the outgroup

The participants evaluated the Albanese on five

scales of semantic differentiation (for ex. Unpleasant/pleasant, representative of the Evaluation Factor. The scale had seven levels: 1 - indicated the negative pole, 4 - was the neutral point, 7 - indicated the positive pole. The five items were combined (alpha = .77).

The aim of this research was to extend the results obtained by Richeson and Shelton (2003), showing that some contact modes have positive effects on intergroup relationships and, at the same time, limit the negative effects of contact on cognitive performance. In particular, the intergroup contact models (Brown & Hewstone, 2005) and the identity of the common ingroup (Gaertner & Dovidio, 2000) were compared: The intergroup relationship that was taken into consideration was between Italians and Albanians.

The hypothesis is that cognitive performance, for participants with high levels of explicit and/or implicit prejudice, is worse when their respective identities are prominent but not when a common identity is prominent or when contact is with a member of the 'ingroup. Furthermore, it is hypothesized that both types of contact (separate groups, common identity) produce positive effects on outgroup evaluations; the effects of generalization should be stronger for those with high levels of initial prejudice, but only when group memberships are prominent.

Conclusions

The results of this research showed that the hypothesis related to cognitive performance, (Stroop Test), is not confirmed. However, there are indications that **cognitive performance** is lower, for those with high levels of explicit and implicit initial prejudice, in the two-group condition, compared to other experimental conditions. This result, however, does not permit us to state that intergroup contact has produced a reduction in the capacity to inhibit inappropriate responses (Richeson & Shelton, 2003). In this case, in fact, we should have found an effect on **cognitive interference**, given by the response times, or by the number of correct answers to the inconsistent items, and not to the suitable items.

As expected, intergroup contact produces **generalization effects**. Both the perception of a common identity (Gaertner & Dovidio, 2000) and the importance of their respective identities (Brown & Hewdtone, 2005), in fact, had positive effects (negative stereotypes, outgroup value). Furthermore, this effect was greater for those with high levels of prejudice, and therefore they were the ones who benefited most from contact. This was true, however, only if group memberships were prominent, that is when the link between the outgroup members present and those not present was more evident (Rothbart & John, 1985). In conclusion, it is confirmed that **contact has positive effects on intergroup relations**. However, the people who benefit most from contact, i.e. those with high levels of prejudice, when group memberships are prominent, are also the ones who tend to have a reduced cognitive performance following an encounter with members of a different group from their own.

*Your mistake is to try to make
your judgments universal.*

Carlos Castañeda

*Which man knows what he has to do?
And knowing it, would be willing to do it?*

George Bernard Shaw

11

SUGGESTIONS FOR EDUCATIONAL STRATEGIES

- *Teaching attention to the individual and overcoming stereotypes*

- *Move attention from the group to the individual*

- *Children from the age of 3 to 7 years are very ethnocentric:* work on emotional processes and try to overcome the good-bad division and bring children closer to concepts and ways of being that are different from their own

- *After the age of 7, children become less prejudice, but social influences increase:* Working on cognitive processes and on attributional style - bringing attention to the similarities between groups and intra-group differences - teaching that two ways of thinking can be different but both are valid

- *Cooperative Learning* (Contact Hypothesis) - working cooperatively in small groups - all members equally contribute to reach the final result - high level student-student interactions - explicit support from teachers

ATTENTION to the *Halo and Pygmalion Effect*. These are uncomfortable topics that I had treated thoroughly in my censored university thesis. Unfortunately, these two factors of a similar nature can jeopardize the reliability of a teacher's judgment on a student's advancement.

Halo Effect

A person who is assessed as a whole, can lead to an altered assessment of the person's attributes. The Halo Effect is defined as the influence of an individual's attitude towards an action based on beliefs about the perceived consequences of the action (Bagozzi, 1999).

The Halo Effect is a term coined by Thorndike to label a psychological attitude which consists of the automatic tendency, during the assessment of a person, to associate a positive quality such as a beautiful physical appearance, to other positive aspects without having any real correlation to that quality, like a nice disposition, intelligence, competence or reliability. It can be considered an important and widespread example of bias operated on a trial and error bases.

Light sheds a halo around an area of dim light, and the surrounding environment is lit by improper light. When an individual's characteristic is illuminated in our eyes, the halo of this light illuminates his personality. This particular feature must strike us considerably because it is the only way that we don't notice that the rest is lit by improper light.

The curious thing is that this effect does not manifest itself only synchronically but also diachronically, that is, the halo does not affect only the rest of the personality, but expands and recedes back to the past, towards everything that the subject in question has achieved.

Physical beauty, the ability to be nice, to resemble, to boast important friends, to know how to praise others and give false compliments, are just some of the ways that many professionals, and non-professionals of persuasion, use to convince us to do things that we would otherwise have never done. In particular it is impressive how important physical appearance is for the purposes of this human and professional assessment. It seems that it is an automatic and unconscious response that we react better to the approach of a person who, for some reason or another, we consider pleasant.

The halo effect occurs when a characteristic of a person dominates the perception that others have of him/her, even with regards to other aspects. It is clear how much it can, positively or negatively, affect the judgment of distorted evaluation formulated by a superior towards an employee, based solely on the obsession of an characteristic of the personality of the latter, which could obscure, in the eyes of the observer, all the positive characteristics of the individual being observed.

Since childhood, we have been taught that it is correct to obey authority and all of society has been ordered according to a principle of hierarchies and laws. This principle is based on an authoritarian hypnosis, charismatic leaders, gurus who claim to hold extraordinary powers, and those who show off their high-sounding titles and, by wearing uniforms try to make the person they are speaking to feel uncomfortable. This explains why in a commercial for toothpaste there is there is a "doctor" wearing his medical uniform who prescribes the purchase of the new anti-plaque toothpaste.

If every type of behavior has a content component and a relationship component it is not even necessary for the authority to be real, it is enough to behave and appear as the holders of an authority over another human being. Some studies have shown a sort of "Halo Effect". In an experiment conducted at a university, a visitor was introduced to different classes, assigning different qualifications each time. As he climbed the steps of the social ladder, the intellect that the students attributed to him also increased (Cialdini, 1995).

The Pygmalion Effect

A study conducted by the University of Oldenburg established that a non-traditional name triggers prejudice (Taino, 2009). A group of researchers led by Professor Astrid Kaiser sent two thousand teachers from the German Grundschule (elementary school) an anonymous questionnaire with very direct questions about personal and educational reactions that different names caused in them. The result is an embarrassing snobbery. The traditional names such as Jakob, Lucas, Simon, Maximilian, Alexander, Hannah, Sophie, Charlotte, Marie by the vast majority of those interviewed, are connected to the picture of a good, disciplined and dedicated student. It is as if the students with the names Giovanni, Andrea, Luca, Giulia all deserved a good grade. Less common names, often chosen after international celebrities, instead provoked an immediate negative judgment in more than half of the teachers: Kevin seems to be the worst for them, but also Angelina, Chantal, Mandy, Maurice and Justin are likely to be rejected before they even start. The prejudice is worrying. But German research touches a delicate point: from the moment it is more likely that families that choose names inspired by television and film stars are less educated and perhaps less well-off, it is clear that discrimination becomes social. Above all, however, the teachers' prejudicial negative attitude weighs on student's performance. Professor Kaiser claims that expectation is the mother of all results.

It has been shown that if a coach does not believe in the potential of an athlete, he/she will not perform to the best of his /her abilities, the same applies to school, if teachers do not believe in the potential of their pupils the performance of these students will decrease.

Particularly in primary school, where encouragement is important, especially in the case of students from immigrant or very poor families who need confidence, but instead encounter prejudice and handicap from the very beginning. The risk that the Kevin's and the Angelina's will forever carry a wound with them caused by prejudice is high. The problem is not just Germany's. Similar studies in the United States have given similar results. And snobbism in terms of names is a reality in all societies with a high level of immigrants and very much influenced by media models: school should however not be a victim.

Psychologists have found that people treat others as they expect to be treated. In other words, those who expect to be cheated are often cheated on, those who live in fear of being abandoned, are often abandoned, those who expect to be betrayed find unfaithful partners. Psychologists have called this correlation, the "Pygmalion" effect.

The Pygmalion effect can manifest itself at school, at work, in a relationship between employer and employees or within the family, in relationships between parents and children and in all those contexts where social relationships develop. Therefore, expectations can affect the quality of interpersonal relationships and the performance of the subjects. Pygmalion, in the myth narrated by Ovid, was a sculptor, he was single and did not have a partner, and therefore had a great desire to give love. His desire exploded one day when he finished a statue of a woman he had worked on for a long time, to the point that he intensely prayed Venus to make him meet a girl who was as beautiful as his statue. Venus, who was moved with compassion, granted his wish, and in the evening, when Pygmalion returned home, he saw that the statue had come to life.

In an elementary school in California, the team led by the American researcher Robert Rosenthal, came up with the idea of an experiment to carry out in social psychology, where a group of pupils undertook an intelligence test (Rosenthal & Jacobson, 1992). He subsequently randomly selected a small number of children, without considering the results and the ranking of the test, and informed the teachers that they were very intelligent students. After a year, Rosenthal went back to the school, and verified that his selected students, who had been randomly chosen, had fully confirmed his forecasts, greatly improving their academic performance to become the best of the class.

This effect, that in in this case was beneficial, manifested thanks to the positive influence of the teachers who succeeded in stimulating in the pupils, as reported by Rosenthal, a lively passion and a strong interest in their studies. The open and stimulating attitude of the teachers helped to develop talents and skills in the children that had been underestimated, up to that moment.

A subsequent research conducted on this Pygmalion effect at school showed that it is due to the different way that teachers treat pupils that they expect the best results from: they behave in a more affectionate way towards them, giving them more time to respond to difficult questions, assigning more demanding tasks to them and more frequently notice and reinforce the activities undertaken independently by these children (Rosenthal, 1994). Ultimately, teachers, consciously or unconsciously, create an environment that promotes better learning for these students, that is, an environment in which their expectations regarding student advancement end up becoming self-fulfilling predictions (Cooper & Good, 1983).

As stated before, unfortunately the Halo and the Pygmalion Effect, two factors of similar nature, can compromise the reliability of a teacher 's judgment on the advancement of a student.

I'd like to tell you story from my high school days. My first two oral tests on philosophy did not go well, I still remember the grades; both D+. Lesson after lesson I was fascinated by the subject and I began to seriously study, it had become one of my favorite subjects. Despite my passion for philosophy my grades over the 3 years, were never more than Cs, except in the last two oral tests during the last year of school when I got a B- and a C+. I still remember very well how outrageous some of the oral tests where. Some of my classmates, in spite of very inadequate preparation, were able to safely get B's, they benefitted of the positive effect of the previous tests. Let's go back to my last oral test, where my grade was C+. I was tested together with one of my classmates who had always got marks between B's and A's-. Although I did much better in the test, she got a B. The "funny" thing was that I was praised for my progress, while my teacher told the other student that she had not done as well as she usually did, she was almost told off for this.

Often when students get bad grades and they justify them because they are persecuted by the teachers, they are only unwilling students who do not accept their responsibilities. However, sometimes, the opposite can happen: especially in pre-school or primary school, often the way teachers feel about their students count more than the objective behaviors of the children in determining the grade of conduct. This is the message perceived by a study carried out by the Manchester Metropolitan University, published and financed by the "Economic & Social Research Council". The British researchers worked with 4 and 5 year old students, paying particular attention to their behavior and to the assessment criteria of the teaching staff.

It was discovered how crucial the first 4 weeks of school are: in that period, the teacher will formulate a judgment that will be very difficult to change, even in front of evidence (MacLure, Jones, Holmes and MacRae, 2008). Moreover, this dogmatic judgment will also be transmitted to his colleagues.

Imagine working for two different employers: employer A and B. Employer A has had negative experiences with his previous employees, therefore he wants to be careful, he does not want to get caught up again. He is convinced he can't expect too much, he thinks that young people are all incompetent, with no desire to work. In fact, he does not have enough trust in you to give you an interesting job, he only gives you small unqualifying tasks. Terrified by the fact that you could be lazy he constantly monitors you, without giving you the least amount of personal autonomy. Moreover, he has no respect for you and tells you this every chance he gets, as well as telling you off for small, unimportant things.

After a few months of being treated like this, in which state of mind would you go to work in the morning? You would probably start to feel de-motivated, start to lose any interest in your work and behave accordingly, you would turn into a lazy and flat employee. So, within a few months, the negative forecasts of employer A would be confirmed. Employer B is by nature an optimist. He expects a lot from you, but he does not ask you for the impossible, he knows you will make mistakes, but he knows that they are part of your learning process. He leaves you a wide margin of autonomy, but at the same time he is always available to give you any suggestions and clarifications you may need. Employer B notices your progress and you feel that your work is recognized and valued also from an economic point of view.

Which employer are you more likely to work with? You would probably produce more with the last one, even if he does not constantly monitor you like the first boss does. Moreover, by comparing the two employers, you can understand why one always finds employees who eventually turn out to be lazy, and the other, on the other hand, finds good employees.

*We should always keep
in mind that numbers are just
a simplification of reality.*

Kenneth Boulding

*Reality is only one way
of achieving the possible.*

Ilya Prigogine

12

EXTRA

Every boat is safer in the port, but that is not what it was built for. I will not always go out into the high seas, and while I fear the storms, I will not go too close to the insidious coast. A substance such as water is the result of the combination of elements like hydrogen and oxygen, and yet it has properties which are very different from both the elements that compose it. The H20 composition does not represent the simple group of its elements but it is crucially determined by their combination. Without the censorship of my university thesis, **"The Theory of Reality",** this book would never have been written. While I wait for it to be published, I would like to pay tribute to it with a short excerpt in this extra chapter. Do not worry, when the right moment comes along, I will publish and tell the whole story in detail and everything will be clearer to you, you will understand, comprehend, and believe me, you will no longer be the same.

In front of the amount and the complexity of information we are confronted with, we tend to reduce our cognitive effort and we use shortcuts that lead us to an approximate and distorted perception of reality. The Theory of Reality by Zeloni Magelli states:

Man cannot know reality. Reality is too complicated to survive in it without simplifying and tidying it, this process involves losing data. This loss of data causes a distorted reality that is different from the original one.

Each of us have our beliefs and even in front of the evidence that we are wrong we tend to deceive ourselves by better remembering information in line with our beliefs and forgetting the information that does not confirm them. Reality therefore becomes our deception, a reality made up of cognitive consonances that previously were dissonances. The wrong perception of reality obviously compromises the reliability of a teacher 's judgment on the advancement of a student and this affects the -school- economy work system, triggering a dangerous chain reaction. Despite everything, this is not a "pessimistic" theory, because in fact it is not so important to know how things really are and to know the reality, the goal of every man is to succeed, trying to achieve happiness and make his own dreams come true.

« Some people will get very angry if we were not able to give a fair judgment, I belonged to that group of people, but I changed my mind. »

Dott. Edoardo Zeloni Magelli

UPGRADE YOUR MIND → zelonimagelli.com

UPGRADE YOUR BUSINESS → zeloni.eu

Biographical References

Adorno T.W., Frenkel-Brunswick E., Levinson D.J. e
Sandford R.N. (1950). *The authoritarian personality*.
New York: Harper; trad. it.: La personalità autoritaria,
Milano, Comunità, 1997.

Akrami N., Ekehammar B. e Araya T. (2000). Classical and
modern racial prejudice: a study of attitudes toward
immigrants in Sweden. *European Journal of Social
Psychology*, 30, 521-532.

Allport, G. W. (1954). *The nature of prejudice*. New York:
Addison-Wesley.

Altemeyer, B. (1996). *The authoritarian specter*. Cambridge,
MA: Harvard University Press.

Anthony, T., Copper, C. e Mullen, B. (1992). Cross-racial
facial identification: A social cognitive integration.
Journal of Social Psycology Bulletin, 18, 296-301.

Arcuri L., Boca S. (1996). Pregiudizio e affiliazione politica:
destra e sinistra di fronte all'immigrazione dal Terzo
Mondo. In: P. Legrenzi, V. Girotto (eds.), *Psicologia e
politica*. Milano: Raffaello Cortina Editore, pp. 241-274.

Aronson, E., Blaney, N., Stephan, C., Sikes, J. e Snapp, M.
(1978). *The Jig-saw classroom*, London, Sage.

Aronson, E. e Bridgeman, D. (1979). Jigsaw groups and the
desegregated classroom: In pursuit of common goals. In
Personality and Social Psychology Bulletin, 5, pp.438-
446.

Bagozzi, R. (1999) Atteggiamenti intenzioni
comportamento, Milano: FrancoAngeli

Batson, C. D., Lishner, Cook, J., & Sawyer, S. (2005).
Similarity and nurturance: Two possible sources of
empathy for strangers. *Basic and Applied Social
Psychology*, 27(1), 15–25.

Benokraitis N.V., Feagin J.R. (1986). *Modern sexism: blatant, subtle, and covert discrimination*. Englewood Cliffs: Prentice Hall.

Blalock, H. (1972). *Social statistics*. New York: McGraw-Hill.

Blascovich, J., Mendes,W. B., Hunter, S. B., &Lickel, B. (2000). Stigma, threat and social interactions. In T. F. Heatherton, R. E. Kleck, M. R. Hebl, & J. G. Hull (Eds.), The social psychology of stigma (pp. 307–333). New York, NY: Guilford Press.

Blascovich, J., Mendes, W. B., Hunter, S. B., Lickel, B., & Kowai-Bell, N. (2001). Perceiver threat in social interactions with stigmatized others. *Journal of Personality and Social Psychology*, 80, 253–267.

Bordens, K. S. & Horowitz I. A. (2002). *Social Psycology*, Mahwah, N.J: Lawrence Erlbaum Associates.

Brewer, M.B. e Miller, N. (1984).*Beyond the contact hypothesis: Theoretical perspectives on desegregation, in Groups in contact: The psychology of desegregation*, (Ed.) N. Miller e M.B. Brewer, New York, Academic Press, pp. 281-302.

Brewer M.B. (2005). Obiettivi sovraordinati versus identità sovraordinata come basi della cooperazione intergruppi. In D. Capozza, R. Brown (eds.), *Identità Sociale. Orientamenti teorici e di ricerca*. Bologna: Patròn, pp.193-214.

Brown R. (1995). *Prejudice. Its Social Psychology*. Oxford: Blackwell; trad.it: Psicologia sociale del pregiudizio, Bologna, Il Mulino

Brown, R., & Hewstone, M. (2005). An integrative theory of intergroup contact. *Advances in Experimental Social Psychology*, 37, 255-343.

Campbell D.T. (1965). Ethnocentric and other altruistic motives. In D. Levine (ed.), Nebraska symposium on motivation. Lincoln, NE: University of Nebraska Press, pp. 283-311.

Capozza, D., Andrighetto, L., & Falvo, R. (2007). *Does status influence perception of humanity?* Manuscript submitted for publication.

Cialdini, R. (1995) Le armi della persuasione, Firenze: Giunti Editore

Coenders M., Scheepers P., Snidermann P.M., Verberk G. (2001). Blatant and subtle prejudice:dimensions, determinants and consequences; some comments on Pettigrew and Meertens. *European Journal of Social Psychology*, 31, 281-298.

Contessa, G. (1999). *Psicologia di gruppo*. Brescia: La Scuola

Cooper, H. & Good, T. (1983) Pygmalion grows up: Studies in the expectation communication process. New York: Longman

Davis, J.A. (1959). A formal interpretation of the theory of relative deprivation. In *Sociometry*, 22, pp. 289-296.

Dixon, J. A., Durrheim, K., & Tredoux, C. (2005). Beyond the optimal strategy: A ''reality check'' for the contact hypothesis. *American Psychologist*, 60, pp. 697–711.

Draine, S. (2003). *Inquisit* (Version 1.33) [Computer software]. Seattle, WA: Millisecond Software.

Eller, A. L., & Abrams, D. (2003). 'Gringos' in Mexico: Cross-sectional and longitudinal effects of language school- promoted contact on intergroup bias. *Group Processes and Intergroup Relations*, 6, pp. 55–75.

Eller, A. L.,&Abrams, D. (2004). Come together: Longitudinal comparisons of Pettigrew's reformulated intergroup contact model and the Common Ingroup Model in Anglo-French and Mexican-American contexts European. *Journal of Social Psychology*, 34, 229–256.

Esses V.M., Dovidio J.F., Jackson, L.M. e Armstrong T.L. (2001). The immigration dilemma: the role of perceived group competition, ethnic prejudice, and national identity. *Journal of Social Issues*, 57(3), 389-412.

Gaertner, S. L., Dovidio, J. F., Anastasio, P. A., Bachman,

B. A., & Rust, M. C. (1993). The common ingroup identity model: Recategorization and the reduction of intergroup bias. In W. Stroebe & M. Hewstone (Ed.), *European Review of social Psychology*, Vol. 4, pp. 1-26.

Gaertner S.L., Dovidio J.F. (1986). The aversive form of racism. In J.F. Dovidio, S.L. Gaertner (ed.): *Prejudice, discrimination and racism*. Orlando: Academic Press, pp. 61-90.

Gaertner, S. L., & Dovidio, J. F. (2000). *Reducing intergroup bias: The common ingroup identity model*. Philadelphia: Psychology Press.

Greenwald, A. G., McGhee, D. E., & Schwartz, J. L. K. (1998). Measuring individual differences in implicit cognition: The implicit association test. *Journal of Personality and Social Psychology*, 74, 1464-1480.

Gurin, P., Dey, E. I., Hurtado, S., & Gurin, G. (2002). Diversity and higher education: Theory and impact on educational outcomes. Harvard Educational Review, 72(3), 330–366.

Gurin, P., Lehman, J. S., & Lewis, E. (2004). *Defneding diversity: Affirmative action at the University of Michigan*. Ann Arbor, MI: University of Michigan Press.

Hamberger J. , Hewstone M. (1997). Interethnic contact as a predictor of blatant and subtle prejudice: Test of a model in four West European nations. *British Journal of Social Psychology*, 35, 173-190.

Haslam, S.A., Turner, J.C., Oakes, P.J. e McGarty, C. (1992). Context-dependent variation in social stereotyping: The effects of intergroup relations as mediated by social change and frame of reference. In *European Journal of Social Psychology*, 22, pp.558-562.

Heitmeyer, W. (Ed.). (2004). Deutsche Zustande. Folge 3 [*The German situation*, Part 3.] Frankfurt am Main. Germany: Suhrkamp Verlag.

Herek, G. M., & Capitanio, J. P. (1996). Some of my best friends:Intergroup contact, concealable stigma, and heterosexuals' attitudes toward gay men and lesbians. *Personality and Social Psychology Bulletin*, 22, 412–424.

Hewstone, M. (2003). Intergroup contact: Panacea for prejudice Psychologist, 16, 352–355.

Hewstone, M., & Brown, R. (1986). Contact is not enough: An intergroup perspective on the "contact hypothesis". In M. Hewstone & R. Brown (Ed.), Contact and conflict in intergroup encounters,pp.1-44. Oxford: Blackwell.

Hewstone, M., Cairns, E., Voci, A., Hamberger, J., & Niens, U. (2006). Intergroup contact, forgiveness, and experience of "The Troubles" in Northern Ireland. *Journal of Social Issues*, 62(1), 99–120.

Islam, M. R., & Hewstone, M. (1993). Dimensions of contact as predictors of intergroup anxiety, perceived out-group variability, and out-group attitude: An integrative model. *Personality and Social Psychology Bulletin*, 19, 700-710

Jaccard, J., Wan, C. K. & Turrisi, R. (1990). The detection and interpretation of interaction effects between continuous variables in multiple regression. *Multivariate Behavioral Research*, 25, pp. 467-478.

Judd, C. M. & Park, B. (1993). Definition and assessment of accuracy in social stereotypes, *Psychological Review*, 100, 109-128.

Kelman, H. (in press). Bridging individual and social change in international conflict: Contextual social psychology in action. In U. Wagner, L. Tropp, G Finchilescu, & C. Tredoux (Eds.), Improving intergroup relations: Building on the legacy of Thomas F. Pettigrew. Oxford, UK: Blackwell

La Barbera F., Andrighetto L., Trifiletti E. (2007). *Stress e videofeedback: uno studio pilota in Italia*. Bologna: Pàtron.

Lee, A. Y. (2001). The mere exposure effect: An uncertainty reduction explanation revisited. *Personality and Social*

Psychology Bulletin, 27, 1255-1266.

Lee, B. A., Farrell, C. R., & Link, B. G. (2004). Revisiting the contact hypothesis: The case of public exposure to homelessness. *American Sociological Review*, 69, 40-63.

Leone L., Chirumbolo A., Aiello A. (2006). Pregiudizio sottile e pregiudizio manifesto: alcuni rilievi critici sullo strumento di Pettigrew e Meertens (1995). *Giornale Italiano di Psicologia*, 33(1),175-195.

Levin, S., van Laar, C., & Sidanius, J. (2003). The effects of ingroup and outgroup friendships on ethnic attitudes in college: A longitudinal study. *Group Processes and Intergroup Relations*, 6, pp. 76–92.

Maass A., Castelli L., Arcuri L. (2005). Misurare il pregiudizio: tecniche implicite versus esplicite. In D. Capozza, R Brown (ed.), *Identità Sociale. Orientamenti teorici e di ricerca*. Bologna: Patròn.

Mancini T., Carbone E. (2007). Identità territoriale, nazionale, europea, culturale e cosmopolita e pregiudizio latente e manifesto. Una ricerca su un gruppo di studenti universitari. *Giornale Italiano di Psicologia*, 1, 117-146.

McFarland, S. (1999). Is authoritarianism sufficient to explain individual differences in prejudice? Unpublished paper delivered at the Oxford, *England meeting of the European Association for Experimental Social Psychology*.

McGarry, J., & O'Leary, B. (1995). Explaining Northern Ireland: Broken images. Oxford, UK: Blackwell

MacLure, M., Jones, L., Holmes, R. e MacRae, C. (2008) Becoming a problem: how and why children acquire a reputation as 'naughty' in the earliest years at school. Economic and Social Research Council

Mendes,W. B., Blascovich, J., Lickel, B., & Hunter, S. (2002).Challenge and threat during social interaction with and black men. *Personality and Social Psychology Bulletin*, 28, pp. 939-952.

Moghaddam (2002). *Psicologia sociale*, Bologna:

Zanichelli.

Moghaddam F.M. (2008). The materialist view: from realistic conflict theory to evolutionary psychology. In F.M. Moghaddam, Multiculturalism and intergroup relations: Psychological implications for democracy in global context. Washington, DC: APA, pp. 65-88.

Paolini, S., Hewstone, M., Cairns,&Voci, A. (2004). Effects of direct and indirect cross-group friendships on judgments of Catholics and Protestants in Northern Ireland: The mediating role of an anxiety-reduction mechanism. *Personality and Social Psychology Bulletin*, 30, pp. 770–786.

Pedersen A., Walker I. (1997). Prejudice against Australian Aboriginals: Old-fashioned and modern forms. *European Journal of Social Psicology*, 27(5), pp. 561-587.

Pettigrew, T. F. (1991). *The importance of cumulative effects: A neglected emphasis of Sherif's work*. In D. Granberg & G. Sarup (Eds.), Social judgment and intergroup relations: Essays in honor of Muzafer Sherif (pp. 89–103). New York, NY: Springer-Verlag.

Pettigrew, T. F. (1998). Intergroup contact theory. *Annual Review of Psychology*, 49, 65-85.

Pettigrew, T. F. (1997). Generalized intergroup contact effects on prejudice. *Personality and Social Psychology Bulletin*, 23,173–185.

Pettigrow, T. F. (2008). Future directions for intergroup contact theory and research, *International Journal of Intercultural Relations*, 32, 187-199.

Pettigrew, T. F. & Meertens, R. W. (1995). Subtle and blatant prejudice in western Europe. *European Journal of Social Psychology*, 25, 57-75.

Pettigrew T.F., Meertens R.W. (2001). In defense of the subtle prejudice concept: a retort. *European Journal of Social Psicology*, 31, 299-310.

Pettigrew, T. F. & Tropp, L. R. (2006). A meta-analytic test of intergroup contact theory, *Journal of Personality and Social Psychology*, 90(5), pp. 751-783.

Richeson, J. A., & Shelton, J. N. (2003). When prejudice does not pay: Effects of interracial contact on executive function. Psychological Science, 14,287-290.

Richeson, J. A., & Shelton, J. N. (2007). Negotiating interracial interactions. *Current Directions in Psychological Science*, 16(6), 316–320.

Richeson, J. A., Trawalter, S., & Shelton, J. N. (2005). African American's implicit racial attitudes and the depletion of executive function after interracial interactions. *Social Cognition*, 23, pp. 336-352.

Rubini M., Moscatelli S., 2004. Categorie e gruppi sociali: alle radici della discriminazione intergruppi. *Giornale Italiano di Psicologia*, 1, 25-68.

Rueda J.F., Navas M. (1996). Hacia una evaluacion de las nuevas formas del prejudicio racial: Las actitudes sutiles del racismo. *Revista de Psicologia Social*, 11, 131-149.

Runciman, W.G. (1966). Relative deprivation and social justice, London, Routledge; trad. it. *Ineguaglianza e conoscenza sociale: l'idea di giustizia sociale nelle classi sociali*, Torino, Einaudi, 1972. Rosenthal, R. (1994). Interpersonal expectancy effects: A 30-year perspective. Current Directions in Psychological Science, 3, 176-179.

Rosenthal, R. & Jacobson, L. (1992) *Pygmalion in the classroom*. Expanded edition, New York: Irvington Publishers

Rothbart, M. & John, O. P. (1985). Social categorization and behavioral episodes: A cognitive analysis of the effects of intergroup contact, *Journal of Social Issues*, 41, 81-104.

Sears D.D. (1988). Simbolic racism. In P.A. Katz, D.A. Taylor (eds.), *Eliminating racism: profiles in controversy*. New York: Plenum Press, pp. 53-84.

Sherif, M. (1966). *In common predicament*. Boston, MA:

Houghton Mifflin.

Sherif M. (1967). *Social Interaction, Process and Products*. Chicago: Aldine; trad. it.: L'interazione sociale, Bologna, Il Mulino, 1972.

Shelton, J. N., Richeson, J. A., & Salvatore, J. (2005). Expecting to be the target of prejudice: Implications for interethnic interactions. *Personality and Social Psychology Bulletin*, 31(9), 1189-1202.

Shelton, J. N., Richeson, J. A., Salvatore, J., & Trawalter, S. (2005).Ironic effects of racial bias during interracial interactions. *Psychological Science*, 16(5), 397-402

Shelton, J. N., & Richeson, J. A. (2006). Ethnic minorities' racial attitudes and contact experiences with people. *Cultural Diversity and Ethnic Minority Psychology*, 12(1), 149-164

Sidanius, J.,&Pratto, F. (1999). *Social dominance: An intergroup theory of social hierarchy and oppression*. Cambridge, UK: Cambridge University Press.

Snyder, M., Tanke, E.D., & Bersheid, E. (1977). Social perception and interpersonal behavior: On the self-fulfilling nature of social stereotypes. *Journal of Personality and Social Psychology*, 35, 656-666.

Stephan, W. G. & Stephan, C. W. (1985). Intergroup anxiety. *Journal of Social Issues*, 41, 157-175.

Stephan, W. G., Stephan, C. W., & Gudykunst, W. B. (1999). Anxiety in intergroup relations: A comparison of anxiety/uncertainty management theory and integrated threat theory. *International Journal of Intercultural Relations*, 23, 613–628.

Stephan,W. G., Boniecki, K. A., Ybarra, O., Bettencourt, A., Ervin, K. S., Jackson, L. A., et al. (2002). The role of threats in the racial attitudes of Blacks and s. *Personality and Social Psychology Bulletin*, 28, 1242-1254

Tajfel, H. (1981) *Human groups and social categories*. Cambridge, UK: Cambridge University Press.

Tajfel H., Billig M.G., Bundy R.P., Flament C. (1971).

Social categorization and intergroup behaviour. *European Journal of Social Psychology*, 1, 149-178.

Tajfel H. e Turner J.C. (1979). An integrative theory of intergroup conflict. In W.G. Austin e S. Worchel (eds.), *The Social Psychology of Intergroup Relations*. Monterey, CA: Brooks/Cole, pp. 33-47.

Tajfel, H., & Wilkes A. L. (1963). Classification and quantitative judgment, British *Journal of Social Psychology*, 54, 101-114.

Taino, D. (2009) La ricerca tedesca: Gli insegnanti non credono negli alunni e il rendimento diminuisce, Corriere della Sera, 20 settembre 2009

Taylor, D.A. e Moriarty, B.F. (1987). In-group bias as a function of competition and race. *Journal of Conflict Resolution*, 31, pp. 192-199.

Tropp, L. R., & Pettigrew, T. F. (2005a). Differential relationships between intergroup contact and affective and cognitive dimensions of prejudice. *Personality and Social Psychology Bulletin*, 31(8), pp. 1145–1158.

Tuckman, B. (1965). "Developmental Sequence in Small Groups" *Psychological Bulletin* 63 pp. 384-399.

Vala J., Brito R., Lopes D. (1999). O racismo flagrante e o racismo subtil em Portugal. In J. Vala (Ed.), *Novo racismos: Perspectivas comparativas*. Oeiras: Celta, pp. 31-59.

Vescio, T. K., Sechrist, G. B., & Paolucci, M. P. (2003). Perspective taking and prejudice reduction: The mediational role of empathy arousal and situational attributions. *European Journal of Social Psychology*, 33, 455–472.

Voci, A.,& Hewstone, M. (2003). Intergroup contact and prejudice toward immigrants in Italy: The mediational role of anxiety and the moderational role of group salience. Group Processes and Intergroup Relations, 6, 37-54.

Williams, R. M., Jr (1947). The reduction of intergroup

tensions. New York: *Social Science Research Council*.

Wright, S. C., Aron, A., McLaughlin-Volpe, T.,&Ropp, S. A. (1997). The extended contact effect. *Journal of Personality and Social Psychology*, 73, 73–90.

Zajonc, R. B. (1968). Attitudinal effects of mere exposure. Journal of Personality and Social Psychology, 9 (Monograph Supplement, No. 2, part 2), 1–27.

Zanon, A. Come le nostre aspettative influenzano le relazioni con gli altri: l'effetto pigmalione (http://www.ilmiopsicologo.it/pagine/come_le_nostre_aspettative_influenzano_le_relazioni_con_gli_altri_l_effetto_pigmalione.aspx) (consultato il 10 Ottobre 2010).

Zeloni Magelli E. (2010) *La Teoria della Realtà.*